Pooping Animals

JUST 4 JOKES
COLORING BOOKS

JUST 4 JOKES
COLORING BOOKS

JUST4JOKES
COLORING BOOKS

JUST 4 JOKES
COLORING BOOKS

JuST4JoKeS
COLORING BOOKS

JUST 4 JOKES
COLORING BOOKS

JUST4JOKES
COLORING BOOKS

JUST4JOKES
COLORING BOOKS

JUST4JOKES
COLORING BOOKS

JUST4JOKES
COLORING BOOKS

JUST4JOKES
COLORING BOOKS

JUST4JOKES
COLORING BOOKS

JUST4JOKES
COLORING BOOKS

Just4Jokes
COLORING BOOKS

JUST4JOKES
COLORING BOOKS

JUST 4 JOKES
COLORING BOOKS

Color Test Page

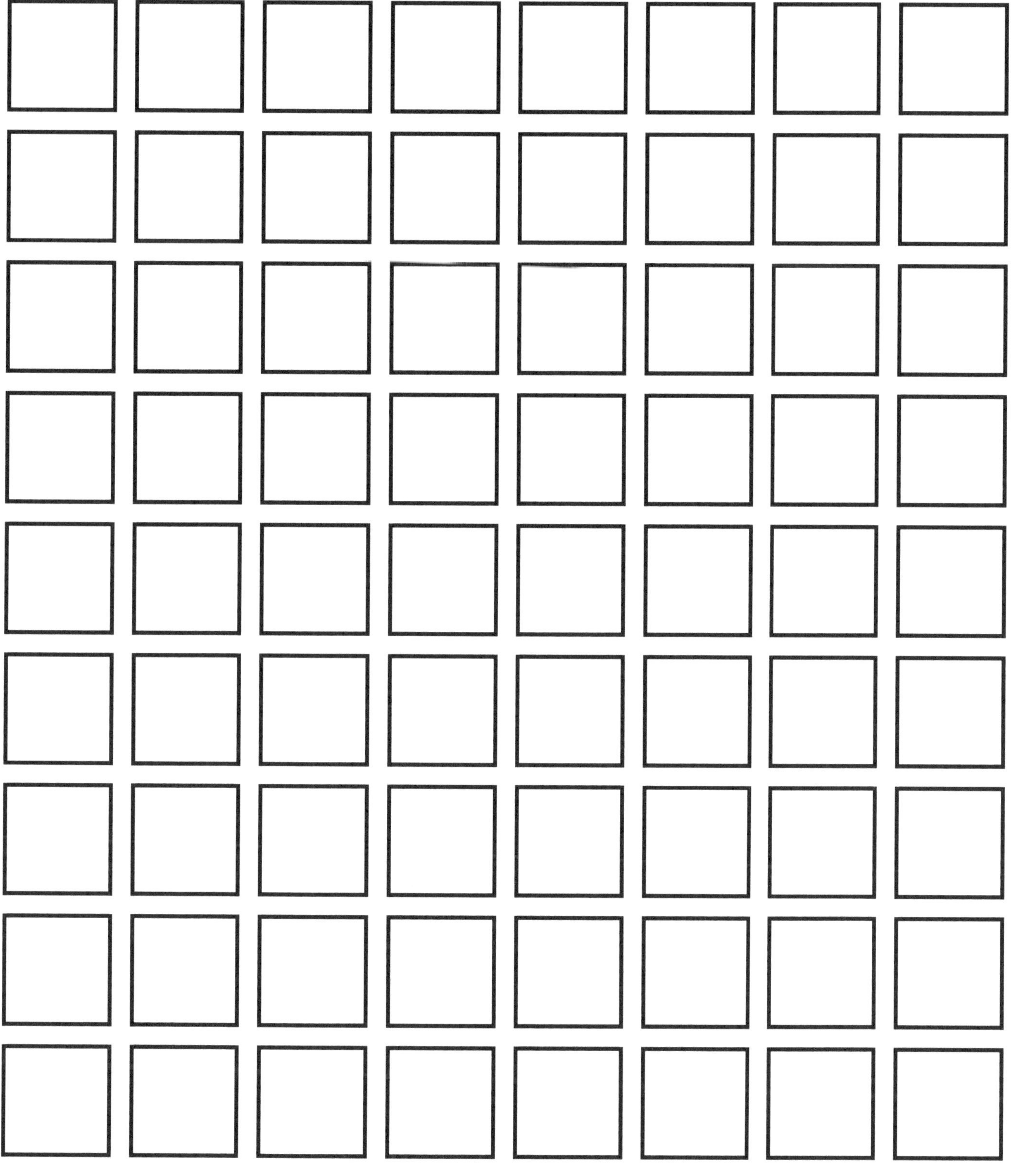

JUST4JOKES
COLORING BOOKS

Color Test Page

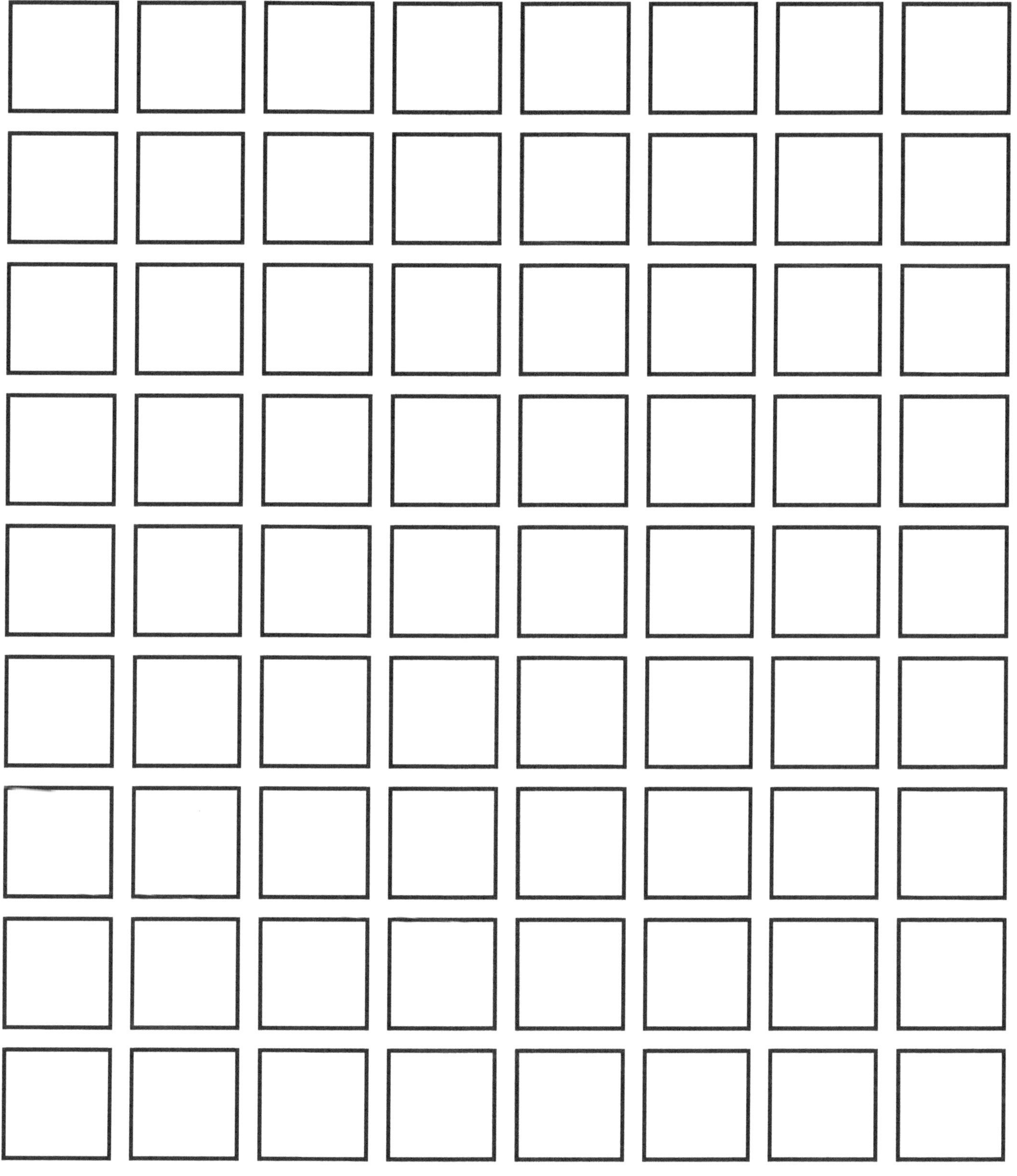

JUST4JOKES
COLORING BOOKS